Natural Affinities

Natural Affinities

Erica Funkhouser

ALICE JAMES BOOKS

The author thanks the following publications in which many of these poems first appeared: *The Boston Phoenix, Dark Horse, Green House, New England Review, The Paris Review, Ploughshares, Poetry* and *Tendril.*

Part Two of "Waiting" has been sandblasted into the new Davis Square Subway Station in Somerville, Massachusetts as part of the *Arts On The Line* program sponsored by the Cambridge Arts Council and funded by the Massachusetts Bay Transportation Authority.

The publication of this book was made possible with support from the Massachusetts Council on the Arts and Humanities, a state agency whose funds are recommended by the Governor and appropriated by the State Legislature.

Library of Congress Catalogue Card Number 82-074512
ISBN 0-914086-43-X (hardbound)
ISBN 0-914086-42-1 (paperback)

Book design by Susan Graham.
Typesetting by The Pressroom, Gloucester, Massachusetts.

Alice James Books are published by the Alice James Poetry Cooperative, Inc.

Alice James Books
138 Mount Auburn Street
Cambridge, Massachusetts 02138

For Thad

CONTENTS

I

II

III

I

BRINGING IN THE SKY

A solitary ibis has the sky to himself today.
His black wings work to bring it down,
the heaviness growing harder
the closer to earth he comes.
His wings are large and long,
but it will be days before
everything visible above the empty trees
is down.
Again and again, the methodical reaper
returns with full loads of sky,
content just to see some of its infinite bulk
beneath him.

TOOLS

HAMMER

The hand is not always extremity enough.
At times we must go farther,
and so the hammer comes to mind.
It leads the strength of shoulder
down through diverse fingers
to a solid head the way
horses are led into canyons,
or thunder.

In hammering, as in domestic matters,
balance determines all:
too little weight
wears the striker out,
too much may mar the stricken.

Repetition is the key, and aim.
Such is the magic of concentration:
every nail slides down
its passageway as if
that destination
had been chosen.

SCREWDRIVER

For those days when drumming
is too direct, a slow twist
of the screwdriver will do.

Descend, descend, whispers the steel
into the little ear
that takes its edge.

Intimate, essential,
the screwdriver to the screw.

PLANE

This one does its work by returning
over and over
to the place where it began
until even memory
bears no splinters.

Flatness, flatness
the plane dreams
as it sweeps down every plank
envisioning unsown fields,
boxcars, Unitarian churches.

"Lie down," sings the plane.
"Lie down and be the same
as all the rest."

PIPE WRENCH

Behold the pipe wrench,
whose vanadium jaw undoes
the smoothest arguments.
It never tastes the copper
or feels the heat nuts reach
before they finally give way.

Impervious to pain, this master.
Undoing its only task.

If eternity had edges, the pipe wrench
would wind time back and never hear a cry.

HAND SAW

Through the soft pulp
of farmed pine, the saw moves
with the incessant logic of progress.

Why stand up when you can fall down?
Why be a tree when you can be a house?
Here there is nothing to hope for
but branches.

As the saw works, it whispers
of soft planks weathering
in lumberyards. It never sees
the nightmares that come to the tree
in the form of windows and doors.

The saw knows only one fear,
the heat of steel
aging as it passes through
throbbing cells.

PAPER CLIPS

They lie flat, their circular tracks
making three turns and finishing
almost exactly where they began.
The paper clips have something to do with me
so I try to read them well.
No, they insist,
they are not trombones to open my mouth;
they are not glass tubes
to conduct my experiment;
they are not paths that lead anywhere.
The words they once held in their thin lips,
whatever they were, are gone now.

EARTH DAY IN PROVINCETOWN

The things we see survived by accident,
are small, happened to be cared for
through centuries of death at sea:
The dollhouse in the druggist's window,
its wives waving as they were seen to wave
in 1810 by the one sailor not at sea.
Imagine what a returning vessel meant to him.

On a red velvet pillow lies an ivory needle
whose scrimshaw bees would scare
the seamstress back from daydream to her sail,
the canvas heavy, resistant on her lap,
not at all like honey,
the delicate collecting of pollen.

On the wall we see what sailors used for flowers
when they rocked, far from any meadow: human hair
braided into blond crysanthemums, black asters,
their sad ability to last forever.
We wonder when the hair was taken from the body.

Is this preservation? In the museum shop
we can buy baby sand sharks bottled in brine
or moon snails mounted as rings,
while outside the museum the drumlin
made by the ache of retreating ice
is once again turning the easy green of spring
as if nothing — not even water — had ever been lost.

THE ICE-FISHING HOUSES

It's November now and the bright wooden huts
with their tiny windows and doors
are afloat on the still unfrozen river.
Their reflections, tangerine and turquoise,
spill freely into the channel —
fishscales, wing-feathers, dust of precious stones.

The life of every color starts in water
startled from these fishhouse walls.
The sun is low and does its shining long,
draws the colors out in brilliant tongues.
Against the fact that winter's on our breath,
we name vermilion, melon, lime.

Close to frozen, the ocean's more a field
where circus wagons stop to spend the night.
We seem to see the fishermen, wrapped in scarves,
laughing among clowns and monkeys,
and not stooped alone over stiff lines
that sink small bait before the eyes of smelt,
hungry and black inside their cold.

LETTUCE

In June, the new lettuce
appears in tidy rows
with the logic of impulse.
The curly heads sit
as if they had landed
during the night
from some outer nebula,
their mere existence genius,
whatever brought them here
irrelevant.

As if a single curve
experienced a single time
were too delicate
even to be eaten,
each head repeats itself
from leaf to leaf.

The inner leaves
are smaller, stiffer,
and the inmost leaves,
receiving the least light,
are all succulence,
their tiny curves
curled around a milky stalk.

WORKHORSES

The whole barn is theirs.
They lean on it,
concentrating on leaning
as they used to concentrate
on pulling, on the habit
of the fields
crossed and recrossed.

Through the hot clapboards
as if through the heat of labor
the horses rediscover
their enormous love
of standing still.

THE THREE-TOED SLOTH

The three-toed sloth
clings to trees
like a very small man
with no ambition.
He keeps
to the deep forest
where no motion
is sudden
and lives alone
nesting
in his own fur.
He needs no home.
He attracts
no attention.
So slow
is the life
of the three-toed sloth,
so nearly like that
of an ancient pond,
that green algae grow
in his thick, still fur.
They settle there
and multiply,
thriving on the sloth's
indifference.
If it were not
for the wingless moths
that visit the sloth
to feed on his coat,
he would become
just another rainforest
close
to extinction.

KEEPING PIGS

The war is over and we're keeping pigs again.
In the heat, the sweet stench of meal
and muck oozes from the pen.

People we meet on trains tell livestock stories:
Italian hogs named Adolf and Benito,
named to spare tears, and two Vermont pigs,
Haldeman and Dean: neat
as stockbrokers, they never wallowed.

Our pigs live like veterans of mistaken wars,
anonymously, rooting out jagged memories.
Millipedes swarm from the sod they overturn,
and the spaces under stones face them
like the gaps left by missing bodies.
They go only so far down
before they hit ledge, shattering
and complicated as motives for killing.

The pigs fatten easily but their scars
swell. No water they drink
remains clear, no straw they lie in clean.

At night I hear them pace and grunt as I sink
into the arms of another soldier,
nicks on his shoulder cool
and streamlined as bullets.

The rain falls around us and turns to mud.
We make a tent of the sheet,
but even here the heavy, nodding faces
push through the surface again.

FISHING FOR FLOUNDER

Whether or not flounder prowl
the floor of Blue Hill Bay
we do not know for sure,
but we lower our knobs of salted pork
on fishhooks as if to ask,

Is it these rocks over which
their flat, white stomachs,
like the hands of the blind,
brush in search of sustenance,
trusting the topography
to take them
where delicious crab crawl?

Is it here their ocean-purple eyes
gaze at the world up as down,
studying its inversions in depth?

We think the flounder must possess
some horizontal wisdom —
the stability of those who never leap,
who stick to the bottom
of life's deep pools.
A bit dull, perhaps,
with their detailed knowledge
of the few bleak centimeters
beneath their gills,
but extraordinarily informed
about the dark motions
whose polished surface
is all we see.

THE WOMEN WHO CLEAN FISH

The women who clean fish are all named Rose
or Grace. They wake up close to the water,
damp and dreamy beneath white sheets,
thinking of white beaches.

It is always humid where they work.
Under plastic aprons, their breasts
foam and bubble. They wear old clothes
because the smell will never go.

On the floor, chlorine.
On the window, dry streams left by gulls.
When tourists come to watch them
working over belts of cod and hake,
they don't look up.

They stand above the gutter. When the belt starts
they pack the bodies in, ten per box,
their tails crisscrossed as if in sacrament.
The dead fish fall compliantly.

It is the iridescent scales that stick,
clinging to cheek and wrist,
lighting up hours later in a dark room.

The packers say they feel orange spawn
between their fingers, the smell of themselves
more like salt than peach.

MARKETPLACE IN OAXACA

i.

The fowl-tender holds a purple gander
inside her black dress.
On her wrists, pairs of roosters
hang by their lashed legs.
Baby chicks, the many folds of her skirt,
move about her waist and feet
as she sits on the wooden egg crate,
lean turkeys at her side like dogs.

ii.

First comes the smell of kerosene,
then the orange wing of fire
shooting toward the sky.
It is the flame swallower.
His only tools a bottle of fuel
and a thin torch, the boy
drinks and then ignites himself
whenever a new crowd draws around.
There is one dark moment
when the flames are sucked inward,
before the explosion
that obscures him completely.

iii.

Here is a box of spun sugar skulls
for the day of the dead or, possibly,
for those on the eve of a journey.
Small as fists, with red foil pushed
into hollow eye sockets
and strands of purple icing for hair,
the skulls are visible everywhere for sale
but we see nobody buy them.

iv.

The girl with the fruit has been trying to catch
someone's attention since dawn.
Pyramids of fresh tangerines
have failed to catch him.
Bananas brought down from the ceiling
with long hooks and released
over the marketplace like swallowtails
have failed to catch him.
Satin woven into her black braids
has failed to catch him.
Now she walks over to him
sitting dumbly behind his table of cooking pots
and plants a shining green parrot on his head.

THE WREN

In the grey morning as the grapeleaves turn
their pale undersides up to dry,
a wren appears, her body ordinary,
but her tail spirited as a baton.
She's dissatisfied with the house hung
in the sugar maple, its roof a white confection,
its doorway an accurate, off-putting *O*.
She'd sooner nest in a goatshed
or beneath a ramshackle bridge.

A lantern-white skull left lying in the grass
like a neglected tool captures the wren's attention.
She seems to recognize the vaulted bones
of a wild fox that paused too long
one snow-bound evening, captivated
by a reverie that lit up every passage
as if with mirrors.

Through entryways that once held tongue and eye,
the wren darts, recalling her first sight of eggshell
from within. Inside, she stops
to reconsider her own small beak,
drab feathers, and there, skittish upon bone,
her particular dream brought home to shine.

THE BLUE IN BEETS

The blue in beets
comes and goes
sometimes a shadow
of the weeds
where beets grew
or of their towering leaves
other times a suggestion
of what the beets
might have been:
blue birds
blue stones
blue fish
blue whales
blue water
If blue isn't here
it's there
if it's not there
it's coming
if you have just seen it
it will be back
if you have never seen it
you will

II

FOR A MAN WHO NEVER DREAMED

In waking life you've seen a red-tailed fox —
that's close to dream, blazing
across the field: hot, fallen star.
Part scent, part singe — its trail.

A dream discovers its own dreamer —
you know a place like that.
Every time you return it's more strange,
more intimate, as if you were getting closer.
Before you see the sea
you remember its black inlet
fits in your hand like a globe of lead,
but later the hand is small again,
empty, and the sea long and flat, beating
at your feet as if it had never been contained.

Those moments in broad daylight, euphoria
close to fear — those, too, are dreams,
when you seem to touch light
and, touching it, receive more than light,
as if you'd found a son inside you.

A dream is just a ghost in search of an equivalent.
It returns each night through the one door
left open. It wears the color of your sleep,
is camouflaged. You have to name
the landscape in detail, examine every branch
until one moves: the dream posing as a mantis.

Try not to think of any ending.
Search instead for pieces —
one girl's shoulder blades cool, walking away from you,
a blue that gives you courage,
work that holds and lightens at once.

At the end of your day,
lie down with one of these in mind.
Envelop it. The seed set deepest
grows most luminous
when you hold on
through its difficult night.

NOTES FROM THE COAST

i.

Remember the river
pulling us in, how we held on
to the uprooted other?

Each time I see you
it's as if you've surfaced
just downstream,

seen something
I'll soon see.

ii.

As you speak I hold
the words, anemones
blown from glass.

iii.

Others fear your beard,
how it hangs,
a weed.

I like the way it swings
beneath your flute.

It makes me think
of the man inside me,
feel my own beard
swaying.

iv.

Don't come to me so often.
I find false comfort
in consistency.

Soon I'll have you made
into a work of art:
steady, perpetual,
cold in my lap.

v.

I try to look empty,
now, when I'm most full.
That way nothing will be taken.

NOT STARS, NOT FISH

On a morning when we're fastened
to the worst that falls
between us, I take a boat
and row out to the starfish
strewn upon their searock
as if tossed down by an archer
who found better gloves to wear.

Body upon body
flattened by wave-press,
the brown and purple stars
cling to each other in heaps:
the opposite of a Japanese garden,
where a few enduring stones
suggest the significance
of time and distance.

I can't decide if the stars are happy.
They're layered deep
from the tide-torn surface
down to their feast of barnacles.
You couldn't map them from the air
or lay them end to end to count them.
Their hunger crowds them down,
exhaustion intertwined with will.

Out from their cramped hearts
I can almost see the five nerves
running toward the dark,
the food that will not move.
They're not stars, although they map
the black cove;
they're not fish
despite their appetite for salt.

And if, right now, they rose to walk
they'd look like star-crossed
lovers: two good legs,
a pair of willing arms,
and one ray more: either a frail
steeple for a head, or the star's
own sex seeking union
with the whole imperfect future.

SALT

In our sea we are the darker waves
that overturn the coast
and scar the sand.
Farther out we are
the fiery ones
shining, not breaking.

Inside the waves we see the rain,
how each drop falls
full of sky.
I find the rain in you
and you in me
before blue is lost
to salt.

We are the salt as well,
the thirst that takes the rain
and makes it float
and age,
float and age.

SEVEN SORROWS

Begin with the sorrow of fields
not snowed on, their bristles
aching and ashamed to lean,
the crows falling
into cold furrows
as if into mirrors.

And then, doors,
how they creak and swell
and never enter any room.
Hands use them and move on.
The two hinges cry and cry.

Or snow, its elaborate hopes
contained in crystals
that land, as stars never do,
complete.

The interior sorrow of clams,
their multitude fervent in mud,
each one waiting for a small
sad ending of its own.

Or sudden wonder,
how the mind is taken,
ignited, left behind.
A blazing stem.

The extended sorrow of porches
where reconsideration begins,
love ends.

And nearby, the neighbors,
the paths beaten down

between houses.
How they fill with rain, with love
wanting to recover its face
in fresh water.

At our feet, the sorrow
of snakeskin, sheer
but empty,
the final dry thrust
that tries to name
itself.

GOODBYE

Today, again, I need you,
but this is no plea to stay in place,
only my way of urging you:
find your new coast quickly,
send word of its detail.

If it's like love, without topography
except for the imagined scene,
then look at the sky instead.
Do the stars shine as quietly
as the moments between embraces?

You'll find water where you're going,
even if your own face isn't there to answer.
In the sour leaf of sorrel
and the salamander at your feet
fleeting vision endures.

In pain, you may discover more.
The two greatest sorrows —
to love, to part with love —
converge as rivers do to make a third shade
of idle blue and disappearing green.

Go quickly, while everything's in motion.
Go farther than love that stops at every border.
Here, the trunks of trees are warm,
their heat rising to a multitude
of amber buds that drop,
like tears, proclaiming:
Praise us. We have been remade.

III

THREE POSTCARDS AND A SEED

From his travels, my grandfather used to send
postcards. Among the pile of letters, they lay
thin as turned leaves, their postage stamps
shining with luminous moths and fish.

The pictures always showed what he had seen:
"This Persian rug was woven by girls
your age. It's the same shape
as the floor of their tent. Those sheep
have their eyes on the high grass
inside the medallion."

On one card, a hand-colored oasis,
brown path between lanes of oil-blue water,
a nomad leaning down to drink, his robe
running into the slow blue Nile.
"Somewhere this river meets the one
behind your house," he wrote,
and I could see our painted turtles
meeting the heavy stares of camels.

Another card said, "Can you say 'makheweyana?'
It means violin in Zulu."
And on the other side, a woman
holding a stick more like a spear,
a beaded cone upon her head.

The last to come was a tiny box
covered in stamps, a note folded
around a deep red pod
that balanced on my thumbnail.
"This opens up," he wrote,

and out spilled nine ivory elephants,
their trunks extended as if to call,
their small backs set
to carry one last load.

NIGHT VIGIL

i.

Nightfall, night air, night owls...
Grandmother watches a different dark.
Her dark. Her stars,
as if she came from there.

"A soapdish! Sawhorses!,"
she cries out, pointing.
My sister and I smell
cold cream, creosote, sawdust.

When milk spills at the table
she says, "The dragon's tail again,"
and nobody is blamed.

ii.

The flowered dress she wore for photographs
wears out, and she begins a quilt.
The phlox and daisies can't keep still.

The pattern: Wedding Star, or Star of Bethlehem.
Bright background is the only new-bought fabric.
She went downtown, asked for "Sunlight Yellow,
Peak of Day." Onto this she sews a star
made of all the dresses he has touched,
her husband, the miner, whose nights
are brighter than his days.

iii.

Daily she waited for the dread caves
to crush her husband.
In the end, he left the mine
when his own lung collapsed.

She bought a Silver Airstream,
drove straight to Tampa.
In one orchard, a stranger asked to photograph
grandfather — the only view we have.
He's holding grapefruits larger than his head,
one in each white hand, momentarily.

iv.

When she died I envied the soil.
Too deep for bulbs, too shallow for coal.

I heard what she said
to the fresh, soft clumps
around her body.

"Where does the grass end, or does it?
Is John L. Lewis far from here?
Do I stay right where I am or will I,
you know, sink a little every year?"

When the soil didn't answer
she began again with stars.
"You see the pick ax next to Venus?
I always loved that little jelly jar,
the one that's clean and empty,
not mine to fill."

50

v.

Earth turns away from her partner the sun
and we call it night.
The eye turns away from her partner light
and we call it final.

I try to find my grandmother's constellations,
but the stars recede like the dull headlamps
of miners descending to a deeper dark.

THREE FEATHERS

i.

My mother calls down the birds
as if her corn were better.
She makes paths through the snow
with her black thistleseed
and all the paths lead to one door
and all the birds come to that door
and my mother stands inside humming:
Evening grosbeak, nuthatch, chickadee.

ii.

Goosedown is the best there is,
she sings, fluffing
our comforters above us.

There is too much heat, we say,
this is like sleeping
under live geese. They slide
away during the night.

Then pretend, she answers,
that you are eggs still warm
inside the hen.

iii.

My mother holds three feathers.
Here, choose...

But I know one feather will draw blood,
another ungrateful children,
the third a loss of memory.

I choose the space between the feathers,
step into it
as into a wilderness
of orphans.

VAGABONDS

"There was once a family who lived in a star
but they had no roof" — my son starts this story
on the way to school, but a donkey grazing
amid snowfall distracts him.
Later, he says his grandfather,
dead nearly a year now, is hiding
in a hole in Egypt, "the one the sun lives in.
He's going up and down with the sun."

Today our northern sun hides behind ice.
We rose and had to wait for light. Zero degrees.
Do you know how the mind goes in search of warmth?
Not forward into deeper winter, but sideways —
crablike, in advance of the equinox, exposing
rigid arms and legs but keeping its face to itself.

Thursday. 5:09 by the clock whose digits
spring like scallions to the dial.
For eight months I have been carrying
a stranger soon to be my child for life.
Do I wander? Am I a vagabond whose sack is full
of clouds gleaned from random scenes?

There's Thoreau sauntering among lichen,
their airy ramifications, and growing sullen
from the weight of his own sanity.
"Who placed us," he asks, "with eyes
between a microscopic and a telescopic world?"

Or, there's Cleopatra, her realm burning
like a star with no roof. As the fire and air rise
she hoists her sails to fly,
leaving behind only the asp's trail
for those who draw conclusions.

54

WAITING

i.

I see word of his arrival
in garden cantaloupe:
thread, strand, branch, root.
The veins in the rind
interweave,
do not break.

ii.

Like a tree that has been chosen
for the owl's home,
I stand up differently today.

iii.

New to the sea, he takes
the shape of rivers
that have just left land:
large with freedom
within a larger body.

iv.

Stiller, laden, I hear more
and from darker corners:
the intonations of his shadow,
mine as well.

v.

A painter now, he works all night
on murals, pigments
seeping far into my walls.

vi.

I sink into deep snow
and feel him, restless underlife,
testing his bulk,
tugging as glaciers must
to cut off cliffs.

vii.

If I'm too wide to walk
through these broad valleys,
how will he pass through
a mouth so small
it doesn't even speak?

viii.

He leaves no room for me
to store my old complaints
and secrets. Out every window
they fly — neighbors and strangers
listening.

ix.

He hurries down at last,
his own Niagara —
glistening, no sign
of the interior.

THE BABY MAKES HIS WAY

The baby makes his way
without a word, with hunter's lips
that fix on openings
I never knew existed.

He surprises like a lover —
only sharper. The novice
breasts can't hide their milk
from tongue and gum and tug.

How he makes it flow,
my unnamed stranger,
as if he had been practicing
on other women.

LIFE STORY

At times the weather doesn't change
so we try to describe our life together:

the man falls asleep
and the baby doesn't

the baby falls asleep
and the man does too

the woman falls asleep
but not the baby

the baby falls asleep
and the woman can't.

The timing's just shy
of the man and the woman
falling asleep together

and the baby not minding at all
because now he's a man
and has all of Flaubert to read
or a mountain to climb
for the first time.

NEW WORDS

My son is two, knows many words, but pronounces
only these perfectly: *shut up* and *fuck*.
They were given to him, like emeralds,
by a wise five-year-old.

"You're not doing it right," I heard her say.
"Make your tongue knock against your bottom teeth."
He practiced with his whole body, his palms
pressed into the rug as if to lift him
up toward *t* and *k*. He could barely breathe
and do as she demanded.

The girl was frantic in her need to teach.
"Grown-ups spit when they say *Shut up*,"
she screamed. "They get you wet."

At home, my son uses his new words reverently.
Pleased to see his dumptruck full of sand,
he holds it high before him. "Shut up, shut up,"
he calls. "I got you round in sand."

Later, he is standing at the window
watching a red bird knock grapes off the arbor.
The bird eats from the ground, his body a larger fruit
among the Senecas and Concords.
"Fuck," cries the boy. "Fuck, fuck, fuck,"
to measure the cardinal's splendid repetition.

If a thing happens often enough, we give it a number.
"Fuck," I begin to count.
"Fuck, fuck, fuck" — a cardinal number,
the number of grapes in a cardinal's meal.
More than ten, probably, less than too many.

DECEMBER, NEW ENGLAND

For the moment the earth's sorrows sleep
below this snow, and joy travels overland
like sunlight over mica, stopping
and entering us at once.
There are no borders or contention.
The rub of ice against water, boulder against bulb,
every impediment from weeds to precedent has vanished.

It's as if no nuclear submarine were being launched
right now in Mystic, Connecticut
beneath a parade of admirals, as if
in New Hampshire workmen from the long-closed
handkerchief factory were not assembling
a grandiose temple to plutonium, their only work in years.

We stand in the interior of a telescope,
a glass channel joining time and space.
This is a world only dreamed of, all its perfections
absences, Utopia: crystalline and temporary
as those moments when a dream's so solid
we step on it and don't fall through.

Suddenly I remember the woman in the market
who was a child in this house, knew the four rooms
when they were layered with pages of farmer's almanac.
She stopped the cash register once to say
she still hears the wind howling through her sleep
as if through that black trumpet on page nine.

Today there are three of us — my son, my husband, myself.
We walk out on the perfect snow as if each crystal

were a maze we've always known the way out of
and all the mazes formed a bridge
to let us travel free of geography and doubt.

Only our son speaks. He has just learned how to question.
"Where are all my countries?," Justin asks,
leaning over the brilliant snow that almost moves
beneath him. He presses his hands into the deep,
receptive white and leaves an archipelago of holes.

POETRY FROM ALICE JAMES BOOKS